Honeyed Ramblings

Jill Forster PhD

IMPORTANT NOTICE

The Honeyed Ramblings

The honeyed ramblings
Of a solitary soul
Roaming the ravines
Of a mind
Beyond control.

Lost its foothold
On familiar ground
Sought to make meaning
Wandered blind...
To love now found.

Alors, contentez-vous du travail comme la fourmi, et du miel comme l'abeille. So be happy with work, like the ant, and honey, like the bee.   Victor Hugo

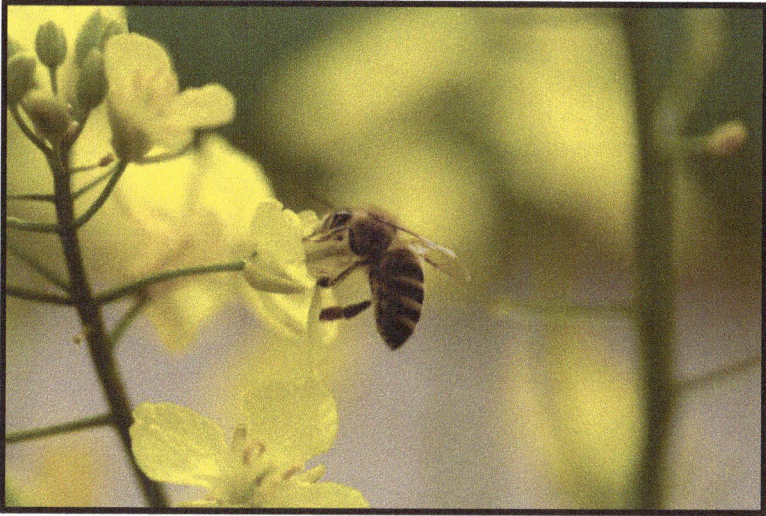

"Honeyed Ramblings" invites readers to ramble through the poems and re-imagine life's joys and uncertainties. The collection of poems brings focus to images such as the watchful heron that hesitates on a railing, the long sweep of tangerine across the broad sky, tête-à-tête coffee conversations, raiding the vegetable patch, travel and cross-cultural coincidence, the light of dawn and dusk, the morning walk, champagne moments and the dusty face of age. The poems help us sway in the sense of the sounds and to listen to the "lull between the waves"- the breath of the heavens themselves . Embracing creativity, we pause to be curious and to wonder at all that is around us whether in human inventiveness or in nature, including the honey bees.

With thanks

To my family – a fine bunch of achievers - I am very grateful. I am their biggest fan and love their care, their humour, their warmth. I wish them fulfilment always, achieving what they most want out of life, most of all happiness. To friends, whose laughs are a major achievement in themselves, I am also very grateful.

For everyone who believes in poetry, may these words ring true in sound and in a sense of wonder whether for bees or beaches or breath itself. To all, especially those who dare to imagine, even perhaps buck the trend, may your ramblings always be honeyed.

To the publishing team – many thanks to Philip Walker for his tireless , good-humoured and helpful efforts and to Philip Mortlock for his ideas and support. Thanks to Alexandra Stellini, graphic designer, for her bee sketches, French chats and for introducing me to a dedicated beekeeper. Credit is due to Michael Mortlock, photographer, for the bee introductory photograph. My gratitude to Jamie Grant, for his editorial insight and comments.

CONTENTS

I

BREATH of HEAVEN

Bee Bourdonnement

Incandescent
Iridescent intuition,
Intense ad infinitum.
Mellifluous murmurings marching
Nature's non-militant emissaries,
Humming harmonies.

Hail the new horizons
That offer up their lotus fare:
Nectar of narcissus and pale perfumed pear
Precious pollen of pomegranates,
Brewing barbiturate balsam
Numbs the overworking senses...lulls.

Sky Breath

Sighing its pleasure
Earthward from the skies,
Heaven stretches smiles
Godliness infused.
Quiet eyes open,
Winds cool the brow
And flutter the psyche.

"Cueillez...les roses"...Ronsard

Cascading Cassia

As light falls
The saffron wisps
Of fragile shards of light
Glow on the crests of cliffs,
Edged with green.

As terns toss
And steer sideways
Chilled by webbed fingers
Of sodden slaps of spume,
The light falls.

Through the sighing whispers
Of slumbers nudged
And muted murmurs
The shimmers slice the memories,
Of other fading days.

Owed to Autumn

The eager, autumn forest thief
In yellow, ragged camouflage
Ransacks leaf by 24 karat leaf
His appetite to assuage.
Slinking in secret stealth
He rips the branches clear,
Stashes ill-gotten wealth
With a smirk that belies his fear.
Concealing the gold-leaf jewels,
In furtive eco-distaste,
With his counterfeit gold for fools
He retreats in irreverent haste.

The Tune of Tuscany

Opening wooden shutters
With all the purpose of the girasole,
Catching sounds of well-intentioned finch-song
Breaking the lethargic day.
Across the horizon in the languid haze
Hearing far- off echoes, breathing the breeze,
Silhouetted towers fill my silent gaze,
Seeing flickered sheen on silver olive leaves.
Waking but entranced by dreamlike smiles,
Over hills and vines and roofs of terracotta,
Sleepy- eyed sunshine soothes and beguiles,
Drowsily attuning to timeless Toscana.

After the Beach

Warmed body,
Salty hair,
Washed skin,
Whitened nails,
Clear-seeing eyes;
Calmed mind
Gazing out.

Rising seas,
Thunder threatens
Blobs of rain
Start to connect
On the wood;
Rainy scents
Fill the nostrils.

Lightning glances,
Frights the horizon,
Sapling sways,
Hail now pelting,
Furied foam
Full of force

Whiteout

At the end of the day that remains
Gazing into oblivion foam
Surround all around.

The Forest Handshake

She walked into the hushed heart of the rainforest
And touched the lichen on the towering tree;
Canopied under the silent symbiosis-
Cool and rich in crush-leafed fragrances-
She waited for the signs of life
Within the light-shy foliage.

The air on her cheeks moist as moss,
Heartbeat now slowed to rhythmic serenity,
Sounds primal and furtive,
Under her feet the matted leaves darkly
Regenerating spores of life,
Distilling a close essence of musk and trust.

So she was eye to eye with the forest creature,
Staring one to the other through the light filter,
Seeking to recognize
Beckoning to identify
Each within
The other.

Cicada Chiaroscuro

"Laissez-nous écouter les cigales."

Takes up position on the line-cut bark
A wood-cut rising in relief,
Apparition in the light so stark ,
Out from the shadow , time so brief.

Through the spotlight glare
Luminous bug eyes peer;
Sounds in high key laid bare
Resonate through shades obscure and clear.

Day's curtains drawn on the mystery
Of the capricious insect-leg spiccato,
Tuning up for the revelry,
Illuminate the cicada concerto.

Day's heat rising brings candescent crescendo,
Chiacchiericcio echoes in shadow turned bright,
Glassy-eyed glissando,
Ecstatic staccato with no respite.

Chilli chimichurri salsa beat,
Contralto clicks, the alto delights,
Rhythmic , free, feel the heat,
Breathe , take in the highlights.

Mariarchi vibration
From abdomen to eardrum,
Anticipation, captivation,
Humming sensation … a bocca chiusa, fast and fulsome.

At last light, shadows descend to lows,
Fading last flourish in cooled cadenza,
The insouciant shimmy slows,
Closing now the promise of cycled agenda.

Not even a whisper;
No more dance feet.
Here today, gone
In a week.

Direction

Gazing out the window
Looking to find what's there,
A full moon on the open sea
Glimmers on the edges
Of the blackness beyond.
The cross extends from the moon's globe
And shows directive signs;
Take any of the four, they'll all lead to heaven,
Just make the sign on your soul
And see where it ends.

II

HUMANITY

Dust

No ranting or whining
Over woes and worries
There's no point
No one is listening...

Can't even pick up the specks of dust
From life's slippery, shiny surface
'Cause they're stuck,
Smeared on for good.

No, time's meandering on
Becomes frozen in the ruts of wrinkles,
Musty in the dust of faces
And greying skin.

And the dust, no, you can't shake it
From the brush bristles it's gripping,
The energy that it took away
It's settled now, inert.

The dust, it's layered on
Over all their scalps
Which start to fester with
What -might-have-beens.

Open the mind's shutters to the full bright
Glimpse, a glint, an ember,
And in the haze of evening light
The dust has settled.

Bye...

We head down the path
And turn, as usual, to wave
And he waves the way old fragile men
Wave when they fear it might be the last.

He picks up the stray leaf
That interferes with the order
Of the tended garden of his mind
Stilled into non-events.

He stands, two feet planted squarely, though not firmly,
On the ground ,
For fear it might-
As with most other things-
Disintegrate.

Cultivated Neglect

The decision is lost in endless revision,
It has ceased to matter
Whether it's the green or the blue
Slippers now, or perhaps the heeled shoe,
Limbs bound, little function
Can barely feel or need the unction.

Gone.

The infinite tenderness of a brother's kiss
That barely touched the cheek
And the heartstrings
That played the hushed melodies of childhood.
The gone forever strains of joy and wide smiles
The still reverberating refrain
Of laughter and salty tears
Of surprise and fears.

The to and fro of the years'
Meaning and stilled moments,
Slumber and walking hours
One flow of fantasy
That makes sense of the not here
That shapes the want to be
And guides the humming
Of the heart's cacophany.

Echoes issue from a lost source
Sonorous and sustained,
Tugs on sleeves of worn out favourites
The lapping of dreamed whispers.
The threads that hung tattered
From the coat's fleece
That shelters from the discord
Of the absent gaze.

Infinitely normal

But for her smile,
Her laugh
From within
From way back
When her world was
Full of joy and promise...
It never kept.

The Loved Ones

I swallow them
Eat them...
But leave them whole,
Masticating every morsel
Or hint of being...
Just to know them.

Futile Conversation

Don't know you at all
Can't get round the wall
Of doubts and indecision
Of irrational revision
Of all the minor points of recall
That don't seem to make sense at all.

Can't piece together the picture
Not free from the stricture,
Can't find the missing link
Can't help but pause and think,
There's no choice at all,
Can only stumble and fall,
No longer need to stall
For time to reveal the meaning...
It's not there, it's gone, no feeling.

Numbed to possibility
Can only guess at the fragility
Of lepidopterous wing
That can make the gentle heart sing
In vibration with its beauty,
Yet alone in its futility.

"Like rearranging deck chairs on the Titanic."

They finger frivolous baubles of frail vanity,
A means of making sense of the day's insanity;
It's a self-absorbed life of chased leisure,
With honeyed, low lights of muted pleasure.

Let's swallow and forget this life's tired troubles
Down another flute, here's to living bubbles.

But tomorrow they can't drink so much,
They're really getting out of touch
With the sane and with the sound,
Just can't go another round.

We have moved to life's raw edge...
And now forgotten what we came for.

God Yul

In the glow of the Christmas toy house
        the warmth
        the smiles
All in miniature.

In the lighted window
        the wonder
        the story
In playthings we believed.

In the red against the snow
        the joy
        the purpose
The essence in play.

By the fireplace
        the comfort
        the contentment
The rocking chair of forever.

Peeping through the window
        the thrill
        the delight
The shining baubles.

Among the naïve dolls
        the gaze
        the connection
Mesmerised in the poem that is Christmas.

The Garden Gnome with Tea and Bickie

His shirt matches the dustpan and broom!
You know that modern teal?
How does it make him feel?
He must feel so very neat
As he sweeps the dust from around his feet.
That twig must go
It's untidy you know.
Look at the grass
It grows so fast,
A millimetre a minute
Clip it and thin it
Like the hedge
With the chopped edge,
The one he stands behind.
But if you look you will find
The gnome in the morning,
On time with the dawning
With tea and bickie
Not one that gets too sticky
Just a little something
Just a little munching
Standing in one's jarmies
Checking the progress of daisies.

Mind's eye

Close your eyes
A child again.
They can't see you.

The Moon Knows

The moon glanced down
And laughed at me:
"Why do you stare?
There's nothing there.
I have told them so
But people just won't let go."

I shield my eyes in thought
And return with the retort,
"How do you dare
Discard my stare?
What do you mean
There's nothing to be seen?
Is that all you can glean?
Where in the world have you been?"

"Then show them to me,
Touch them, hold them,"
Squinting through the glare,
Hiding from the stare,
The righteous moon replied with glee,
And sniggered, "Well then, you see?"

The sense, the substance,
No artful misleading,
I had read with care,
So I held the dare,
And turned from the light to kiss your lips
Then turning back quickly without reprieve:
"Here it is, here it is, now do you believe?"
                    ...and the moon just stared.

No More

A tear rolled down the slope of time.
It hung a while, a crystal of strife.
It had been to that place,
Now it will run no more.

It falls in its searching
For the very end
It has reached the shore...
Where bleached shells remain.

Tears to Laughter

Echoes of sadness
Welling up with tears
Reverberating pain,
Let me take their salt on my own tongue.
Trade tears for tenderness,
Touch devoid of sorrow,
Thrilled now to laughing echoes,
Welling up with joy.

Urge to be Whole

Escaping from the dark
And obstacles too stark,
The stars shone bright on what could be
On eternal, incomplete impossibility.
No need to feel defeat,
Only to be replete.

Morning Walk

So I still have to climb
All these hills,
And sweat,
And then some more,
And thirst and pant,
Some 218 steps, and all puffed.

But you've already finished
And swum
And stretched,
Showered off the salt,
And you're clean
And all coiffed...

The Last Breath

Inspiration - different from aspiration -
   The first I take as a deep life-giving breath
   The other going to a higher plane, so different from
Respiration which is surviving... or not.
This is the lull between the waves, between breaths –
A moment, a reflection, an essence, a lingering...

The crossing over - never 'til now saw it as exactly that –
   Moving from the here and now to there and then;
   Whatever it is, just let me make the leap,
I'm exactly on the edge;
Don't let me open my eyes anymore
If it's to see you and so
To know I'm still here;
Let me go.

And that so-called leap-
   One that requires no quadriceps or calf muscles
   Since I don't have any-
Is onto the ebb-floating boat
Poised effortlessly on the tide
Which we know, waits for no man.

But wait I am no-man, that's me,
You have indeed been waiting for me;
And it will take me no effort to board -
I'm just drifting and my body no longer gets in the way.
Rhythms have gone
No striding or pattern, just adrift.

And so I now see in my mind's eye,
   Since eyesight is no longer mine
   And where did they put my glasses anyway?
That rhyme is not always important
But vision always is
Even while the meaning remains fluid, afloat and now …
Forlorn.

Making Mead

Drifting in on the morning air
The gauzed light
Silhouettes her wings
Drizzled with the honey droplets
Of contentment.

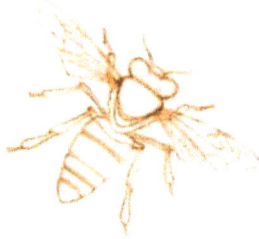

III

UNRAVELLED

Where's the Weft

Rabid , rampant ramblings
The insights of a madman,
Unravelling.

Thread

I've lost the thread.
Been misled.
Entangled in the weaving,
Lost touch with the meaning.
Can't see the design,
Can't see its colours and scope,
Don't have a hope,
Can't feel the weft,
Have to become more deft
… At making new patterns.

The Mind's Faeries

The faeries wander untamed through her mind,
Lucent, feathering lucid eyes shut blind,
Whispering, sighing sweet psalms in her ear,
Sibylline secrets no humans can hear.

They climb over worn out hillocky hope,
Meandering among scented heliotrope,
Steeled by the glints of un-mined troves,
Trampling past holy waters into darkened groves.
With sugared incantation, their trysts sealed,
The dragon's cauldron den is now revealed:
Its fired breath the sightless scorches,
And the faeries ring their torches
Round her lonely plaintiff plight,
Their magic shows its menacing might.

Their lilting voices soothe the weeping lost
Whose eyes through fairy frankincense are glossed
With floss of dreams that have led her far away
From murmured truth eternally to stray.
Lurking , they caress damp air without sound,
Hammer hard gnarled roots of despair's dank ground.
Breathless they hear their heartbeats pound in time,
They wail, gyrate and jive in metred rhyme.
They pursue the shadows, seeking shelter there,
Restless, eager energies spent, her soul standing bare.

They touch coloured ripples of sunlight
Russet gems of ripened berries bright
That weigh down the raven's branches
And cheeks' sanguine colour blanches;
The jewels of delight that dazzle,
Silken locks bleach gold and frazzle,
The tired tremor of the ember
Of long-spent gleams she can remember,
Out of beatific booty they give birth
To unparalleled and mythical mirth.

After seduction, the sinister siren snigger,
Only to understand that it's the trigger
Of haunting hunger never sated,
Lingering actions now too belated.

Bathed in musked and mellifluous malice,
They drink deep from the iconoclast's chalice.
Their honeyed fingers trace the eyes' rims
They blink and wink and a pale light dims.
Then the slow, rhythmic dance
The long-lasting trance...
They lay their bodies on cushions of lust
Sprawling lethargic, loose limbs in the dust;
They reveal their unexpected grin
At the spirit's unanticipated sin.

You see you could have resisted
Having your sight scorched and blistered
By the fierce barbs of their fey fury
...Tricking forever your mind's jury.

And then the faeries they came again...

Wild and furious in their demon dance
Seeping wounds they intend to prod and lance;
Silken lascivious strands of harpies' hair
Lashing at every haloed, craving care,
They shrouded any whisper of light
Failed to ease this infected plight.
With unrelenting barren beat,
They stormed and stamped their fragile feet
To know what it was she wanted,
Shine the light on all that daunted.

Their burning fury smelted every mood
...But in their weightless wrath they are so shrewd.
Be sure to hide away and to shun the glimmer,
Raise the faery barrier, the light grows dimmer,
Close the shutters, you'll keep it out,
Darker now, there is still the doubt.
The serene sense of here and now
Can gild the furrows in the brow,
The protecting glare of the brazen cross
Utterly purifying the soul's dross.

Leaves of chalcedony in rainbow prisms
Shining light on the prophetic schisms,
On spangled weaponry that piously divides
And all idle intentions in the heavens hides.
Like the rising tide of the star-filled sea,
Its fall will be endless, so says the Chaldea.
The soothing chrism confirms belief,
To be sure and certain would lend relief.
Smirking, sneering with frail- fingered unction,
The faeries have vanished her compunction.

Murmuring certainty of there and then
Could have shifted forwards to the mind's Zen.
Hovering in the dulcet, deceiving scherzo
Makes the mind wander in its own intermezzo
With the maybe of duty and desire,
Placing righteous decision on the pyre.
The ethereal fire burns through fugal resolve
To melt at counterpoint and slowly to absolve,
It unfurls its flame, flickers and enchants
Becomes a dulled dervish in blessed trance.

But you can never close the unlocked door
Now ajar -   you'll always be seeking more,
The fierce faeries have entered your mind,
They have left their swollen footprints behind.

In the Web

On the outer edge of the web,
The most fragile
The least connected place,
A tenuous hold
So far from the centre,
So much on the edge of making sense
Of the pattern, of the whole.
And there the spell-maker weaves some more,
Draws inwards; the pattern shrinks,
Becomes intense,
Entangles.

Mesmerising the Muse

Call on the muse
Freed tresses falling
Loosened and spirited;
Cajoled, caressed , courted,
Bring her rambling spirit
Into direct pursuit.

Lure out the lyre-song
With siren notes that ring true
In verse that sings of alluring glories
Chiselled in sea sculptures,
Furrowed tales of heroic certainty
That in truth you must simply be.

Meaning- Maker

Weave the untied threads of gold
Across prophecies untold.
Entwine the myriad fibres
Among the hearts of survivors
Who, intent on pursuit
Chase rhymes they can refute
And rhythms of harmony
To live in the endless melody,
With passions both new and old
The myth has begun to unfold;
Past and future revelation
Connected in a precious creation.

Let it Shine.

Tell me what it is that you want
And I'll fetch it.
I'll bring it to you straight today.
For the longing in your eyes
Tells me you must have it
I'll send that hankering away.

Tell me what it is that I must have
Bring it to me in all its delight.
The truest thing, the one I crave.
Climb up the ladder and pluck out the star so bright.

Send away all the yearning
Dry the tears, move on;
Shining stars have us still learning,
They shine to light up what there is
They cannot lure to what's not there.

Tinker, tailor ... muse

He's in there clattering pots and pans
Sorting ingredients for convoluted plans
Tinkering among the heart strings
And the I don't cares,
Rearranging flotsam cringe
From bygone dares.

Rattling among the clutter
Muddling through the inchoate
Baked on caramelled shreds,
Rummaging among the rough ends
And spun sugared threads
Stitching them all up into patterned sense.

Cross-Hatched

With particularities and sensitivities
With insecurities and counterfeits
Wide gaps, warp and weft
Repetition
Repetition
Narrower gaps
Narrowing
No sense
No light
No gaps
No
Love.

Bee Politic

Blessed bountiful bees' produce
Its purity we cannot reduce
For fear we contaminate
A wholesome distillate
Of toil and perseverance
And diligent adherence
To all that matters,
Laid out on platters
That ooze with sweet soothing
Created with crooning
Hums of delight
Buzzing with might
Have- beens of innocent
Manufacture, now spent.

IV

LIFE'S DANCE

Webbed Prayer

To seek is what it can share,
To give is what it seeks,
In spiralling whispers it speaks.
Riches of itself, so rare.

Tracing in the air
The faltering forms so bright,
The threaded wisps of light,
To see it can hardly dare.

Reaching out to show its care,
To want to hold,
From shadows unfold,
And commune in webbed prayer.

On Reflection.

Take her to the beyond
To see the fairy pond
And spy on her reflection
The child and woman, in introspection.

Relentless rhythms

You can't shut it down
The relentless manufacture.
The words stomp through your skull
With never-ending prattle.

Turn it down
Make it slow
Jot it down
Stem the flow.

Call and Beckon Beyond

The balance, the fall,
The beck and call,
The trust, the recoil,
The honesty, the foil.

> The arch in the sky
> Dips down in delight
> To soar with colours of joy.

The essence , the fact,
The spirit, the touch,
The purpose, the track
The scheme, the line.

> The foam on the shore
> Rushes forwards and back....
> To return with a laugh.

Never-ending

"The end is where we start from".
With every heartache, the exquisite joy
Of being reborn,
A spiralling return
Onward but ceaseless
And back again.

"But where is the beginning?
Sail on and when it's done
The voyage has just begun.
When the tear begins, it has already fallen
In the waking dreaming
Is the end.

Prayer to Harmony

Put me back on an even keel

Comfort me, joke with me

Let me see what's real.

Count my blessings

Over the wall,

See the spirit

However small;

Know the perfection

The infinite giver

Of all that delights

The infinitesimal shiver

Of the softest petal,

The finest web

The craziest hum,

The flow and the ebb

Which together will take me

To the ultimate point

Where the showers of rejoicing

My soul anoint.

The Everlasting and the Everfleeing

One always to be held
The other onwards compelled.
One forever truths has taught
The other's truths never to be caught.
One filling the senses
One leaping over the fences.
One reality displacing
The other life outpacing.

Languor

The lulled lustre

On the outward rush

And the returning stilled hush,

I breathe in the lilting light of the waves.

White Noise

It's not white really
Unless you mean the white of clouds
The white of wan smiles
The white of whitewash
The white of the ocean spume...
But it surely cocoons
Secures your thought flow
Cuts out the static.

"The dance is all there is."

Dance on , dance on,
Caress the rhythms
Swirl with the tune
Sing out the rhymes
Dream in the swoon
Play on play on
Just need to croon
In notes of harmony.

Where is it?

Between the ebb and the flow
The silence.
Between the hesitation and the embrace
The shiver.
Between the surge and the dying
The ecstasy.
Between the trouble and the force
The release.
Between the passion and the pain
The reality.
Between the ground and the moon
The exception.

Immersed in the silence, warming with the shiver,
Exalting in the ecstasy, rejoicing in the release,
Treading the reality...seeking the exception.

A Shower in Winter

Humming in the warmth,

Suffused through the body,

Plumping the skin,

Eyes closed with rejoicing,

Cells brimming full

With the mirth of moisture.

Floating Dreams

Hold onto the dreaming
A moment in time,
Silent gaze still lingering
Beyond the daylight mime.

Float away on the azure,
Drift on the rising tide.
Forget to measure all meaning,
Just take sense from the wave's ride.

Glide way out into the emotion
Beyond chrysoprase lows and highs,
Ease out towards the horizon
And look for it in my eyes.

Travel Safely

Should we have known something more when she left?
Something unknown that left us so very bereft
Of far-sighted purpose and fixed resolve,
Though now the *je ne sais quoi* can evolve
Into something which in the heart will still linger,
The drawn out melody of the lonely siren singer.
The streamers off the side of the ship soon to set sail,
A symbol of joys in the traveller's tale
That croons of the wonder of far-flung places
But etches with care the cultivated lines of our faces;
Rocking on the swell, far-gazing seaward
Something haunting, lurking leeward
It surges with the need to belong
And recalls the strains of an older sea song,
Searching for something else to woo;
When you leave me, should I come too?

Santé

Champagne chimera over the sea,
Bubble-filled flute,
Here's to life's revelry.
Floating to fading
On the dimmed light of memory,
Soft smiles sinking
Fusing a simple fantasy.
Languorous laughing,
Beyond time's reverie.

V

MEANING in MINUTIAE

One Tern Deserves Another

    — *Come fly with me*,
I'll take you to lands
You'll love to explore
And soar into heavens
Where you've never been before.
And wing over currents
That stir and exhilarate;
Wheeling out from shore,
Take a chance on fate.

    — *I'm just pecking at grit*,
Claws tucked in the sand
Here there's nothing to fear,
I'm secure on the ground,
Just puddling through another year.
Stop swimming across the current
Keep oily feathers saturated,
I don't truly need to be 'found',
Nor have peace of mind recreated.

Sugar Feet

The dancing camaraderie all around the pantry
Overflowing with ant-like hilarity,
With sugared tips on formic feet,
High on glucose and raw ant meat.

They have feasted for days and days
On sugary cubes they've grazed,
Hiding in cool dark crevices,
Lurking on laminate precipices.

Tittering and tottering on high-heeled merriment
With packet combinations they blithely experiment,
Shoving and pushing for each and every morsel
Sneaking away with their precious, sickly parcel.

The creaking door left ajar will reveal
Faint snickers after the addicts steal,
There's nothing to see but bodily repartee,
Secret footprints of treacled glee.

Gregarious Ligurians.

To my Valentine
Hope you will forever,
And truly, be mine,
Toeing straight together
Life's challenging line,
Storms and never-never
Or cruising on Cloud Nine.

And when smiles don't quite rhyme
Even when days lack rhythm,
Moor in a halcyon clime,
Keep hearts in equilibrium,
Taking sundowns at a time
Leeward coasting ligurian,
Drift in a becalmed mime.

Hors d'oeuvre of Ravishing Radishes

Wrenched from the fecund bed,
Tendril sprouts filled with dread,
Roots shaken dirt-free,
They gasp with a silent plea.
The looter astride the vegetable patch,
Smiles at his winter cache-
Resplendent in colour and form
The radishes our plates will adorn.
Triumphant he tends to his spoils
With salt and unguents oils
He staunches the sapped fervour
To produce his exultant chef-d'oeuvre.

Cross-cultural Citrus

The tradition of the orange in the Christmas stocking,
why is it there?
...Let's not forget to keep our yearnings in check.

Oh Orange of the Orient
Having travelled far
Precious Ottoman present
Or frankincense and ...
We demur from all truism
To tell what's in our hearts,
Golden Sanskrit of healing prayer,
Infinite repetition in the eastern skies.
Spiral peeling its power
To the tall heavenly tower,
Of truth through object sentient,
Of simple, sweet enlightenment.

Vermilion dawning of a closed revelation
Magenta that bleeds its musings,
Beneath the hallowed horizon
Highest heavenly sphere,
Celestial orb of goodness
With yellow-red juices
Of crepuscule crush
Fleetingly sustaining,
Nourish body, heart and mind
With ruby globules pay in kind
Global understanding and fullness
Of hearts and boundless munificence.

A godly gate opens to the empyrean,
Prophets progress with Byzantine bounty,
Cravings across the cerulean,
Wrapped in darkness
Under a star and crescent moon,
Nimbus halo eclipses our restless souls.
The warmed cheek blush,
Beneath the mantelpiece,
Smiles across the magic storied
Globe of fire, saffron spheroid,
A hidden Zen keepsake
For love of life's sake.

By shining compass
Benevolent duty pays
Ebullient Saint Nicholas
With coins as bullion barter,
Trades for jangling laughter,
A babble of exchange,
Language beyond Babel;
For the tangerine titian- haired cherub
'Tis the joyful season
Of real rind and reason,
Breathe in its skin,
The zest for life, kith and kin.

Hummingbird Hovering.

There it is in essence,
But it won't be held.
The measured wings,
Aligned to the resonant air,
Beat to make meaning
And hold true.

Ligurian Lover

A poet, a coast, a bee
-More humble
Than the bumble-
But truly love all three.

Who will be the bees' keeper?

Bee Business

Mead of meaningfulness
And sense of purpose,
Byte of blessed wisdom,
Belonging and bliss.

Drone in the pattern,
Biding tethered time
To mission accomplish
In foraging flight.

Hum of the helicopter
Over buzz-winged delights,
Fly back in the swarm,
Vibrate the beck and call.

Home in from the horizon
Satellite senses tuned,
Measured beeline to the matrix,
Fluctuate in viscous cells.

Minuscule alchemists
Hover in liquid licence
On pots of nectar gold,
Priceless pleasure pursuits.

Wings oscillate
In the honeyed light,
Bee legs dance in the honeycomb -
The mull of murmurings.

Jill Forster

Inspiration and imagination, these are vital to poetry and to life itself. With this as an essential belief, Jill Forster has produced another volume of poems, *Honeyed Ramblings*, in addition to her first poetry volume, *Lullabies.* With honeyed threads of ideas and imagery inspired by really seeing and listening to all that is around us, *Honeyed Ramblings* weaves its way through musings on life and its meanings.

Jill Forster, PhD in educational psychology and curriculum, has taught at schools and lectured at universities, and is currently an educational speaker, consultant, adviser and writer. In addition to her poetry books, she has written *Think about...Creativity* and *Think about...Mentoring.* Her numerous published educational articles promote classroom challenge and creativity in our thinking across all fields.